About the Urban Land Institute

The mission of the Urban Land Institute is to provide leadership in the responsible use of land and in creating and sustaining thriving communities worldwide. ULI is committed to

- Bringing together leaders from across the fields of real estate and land use policy to exchange best practices and serve community needs;

- Fostering collaboration within and beyond ULI's membership through mentoring, dialogue, and problem solving;

- Exploring issues of urbanization, conservation, regeneration, land use, capital formation, and sustainable development;

- Advancing land use policies and design practices that respect the uniqueness of both built and natural environments;

- Sharing knowledge through education, applied research, publishing, and electronic media; and

- Sustaining a diverse global network of local practice and advisory efforts that address current and future challenges.

Established in 1936, the Institute today has more than 34,000 members representing the entire spectrum of the land use and development disciplines. ULI relies heavily on the experience of its members. It is through member involvement and information resources that ULI has been able to set standards of excellence in development practice. The Institute has long been recognized as one of the world's most respected and widely quoted sources of objective information on urban planning, growth, and development.

Project Staff

Kathleen Carey
Chief Content Officer

Maureen McAvey
ULI/Bucksbaum Family
Chair for Retail

Stockton Williams
Executive Director
Terwilliger Center for Housing

James A. Mulligan
Senior Editor

Joanne Platt
Publications
Professionals LLC
Manuscript Editor

Betsy Van Buskirk
Creative Director

Arc Group Ltd
Graphic Design

Craig Chapman
Senior Director
Publishing Operations

Cover photo:© Lise Gagne/iStock

Recommended bibliographic listing:
Lachman, M. Leanne, and Deborah L. Brett. *Gen Y and Housing: What They Want and Where They Want It*. Washington, D.C.: Urban Land Institute, 2015.

ISBN: 978-0-87420-364-6

©2015 by the Urban Land Institute
1025 Thomas Jefferson Street, NW
Suite 500 West
Washington, DC 20007-5201

About UDR

UDR Inc. (NYSE:UDR), an S&P 400 company, is a leading multifamily real estate investment trust with a demonstrated performance history of delivering superior and dependable returns by successfully managing, buying, selling, developing, and redeveloping attractive real estate properties in targeted U.S. markets. As of March 31, 2015, UDR owned or had an ownership position in 48,086 apartment homes, including 1,434 homes under development. Thomas Toomey, president and chief executive officer, and Jerry Davis, senior vice president and chief operating officer, generously supported the research and advised on the report content.

About the ULI Foundation

The ULI Foundation is the philanthropic partner of the Urban Land Institute, providing an assured source of funding for ULI's core research, education, and public service activities. Through its various giving programs, the Foundation helps strengthen ULI's ability to provide leadership in the responsible use of land to enhance the total environment.

Additional production and editorial support was provided by the ULI Terwilliger Center for Housing.

Urban Land Institute

Terwilliger Center for Housing

About the Authors

M. Leanne Lachman is president of Lachman Associates, a real estate consulting firm serving private and institutional investors. She is also an executive-in-residence at Columbia University's Graduate Business School and serves on the boards of Liberty Property Trust and Lincoln National Corporation.

After an early career in market analysis with Real Estate Research Corporation, where she was president and chief executive officer for eight years and initiated the *Emerging Trends in Real Estate* publication, Lachman moved into portfolio management for pension funds. She spent 13 years as a partner with Schroder Real Estate Associates, which was sold to Lend Lease Real Estate Investments, where she was head of real estate strategies.

Lachman is widely published and is a frequent speaker. She is a ULI trustee and governor; is listed in *Who's Who in America*, *Who's Who in Finance and Industry*, and *The World Who's Who of Women*; and received the James Graaskamp Award for pragmatic real estate research in 1997 from the Pension Real Estate Association. She was awarded a BA from the University of Southern California and an MA from Claremont Graduate University.

Deborah L. Brett is a real estate and planning consultant for a wide range of public and private organizations, providing project-related market analyses. Areas of specialization include development planning, commercial revitalization, market-rate and affordable housing, mixed-use projects, and transit-oriented development.

Brett formed Deborah L. Brett & Associates, based in Plainsboro, New Jersey, in 1993. She previously served as senior vice president and director of consulting services at Real Estate Research Corporation in Chicago. In her 18-year career there, she directed land use policy studies for many government agencies and prepared development strategies and analyses for private clients.

Brett holds a master's degree in urban and regional planning from the University of Illinois at Urbana-Champaign. She is a longtime member of ULI and a frequent contributor to its publications, including *Real Estate Market Analysis: Methods and Case Studies*, used by real estate and planning programs at many universities. Brett is also a member of the American Institute of Certified Planners and Lambda Alpha, the real estate and land economics honorary society.

Dr. Lawrence Becker provided assistance in survey design, sampling, and statistical analysis. He holds a PhD in social psychology from the University of California at Davis and has extensive experience in market and advertising research.

Introduction

The Millennial/Gen Y population is now 20 to 37 years old and continues to fascinate demographers and business planners alike. What will they do as they age? Will they really be just like previous generations—only more tech savvy—or are they really a different generation with some fundamental value shifts. From a real estate perspective, what are they interested in buying or renting? Are they as urban as the media might have you believe, or will they migrate to the suburbs as they have children and worry about schools, backyard play areas, and space to store soccer balls and other gear. They remain the largest demographic cohort in America and a buying force for products of all types. Within the real estate community, their size alone encourages us to study the group in detail.

As a follow-up to the ULI's 2011 report *Generation Y: America's New Housing Wave,* a survey was conducted in November 2014. A review of what has changed and what trends held true provides fascinating reading and offers opportunities for new corporate strategic planning. The subtitle of this report is "What They Want and Where They Want It." It's all about choice. Wise developers and investors will realize that the diversity of Gen Y members means they will demand and seek ways to achieve just exactly what each individual wants. While homeownership is still desired by this group, many remain renters and face economic challenges. Multigenerational households are a factor: many Gen Yers still live with their parents and continue to be slow in establishing their own households. The report contains many more insights and facts to ponder.

M. Leanne Lachman and Deborah Brett created the survey and developed the analysis and insights so critical to anyone working in this arena. Their deep understanding of the real estate field provides a broad context for the study findings and good recommendations to consider.

ULI wishes to acknowledge and express gratitude for the generous support of UDR Inc. in making this report possible. Both Tom Toomey, president and CEO, and Jerry Davis, senior vice president and chief operating officer, enthusiastically engaged in considering new study areas as well as how to revisit questions from the 2011 report.

We hope this publication will again spur lively dialogue and interest across all ULI platforms and networks.

Contents

UDR invests in, develops, operates, and manages a wide variety of multifamily homes in select markets across the United States. Its mix of units and lifestyles is indicative of the array of housing products that appeal to the Gen-Y demographic.

Executive Summary

Members of Generation Y (or Millennials) are an intriguing combination of optimism and realism: virtually all expect to own a home eventually, yet they are not particularly positive about housing as an investment. The features they covet are the extra space, privacy, and predictability of monthly cost that come with homeownership. Almost nine of ten Gen Yers expect to match or exceed their parents' economic situation over their lifetimes; yet 21 percent still live with their parents or other older relatives, and, of those, almost half moved back home after having lived independently.

This survey was conducted in November 2014 when Gen Yers were 19 to 36 years old; this year, they are turning 20 to 37. Totaling 78.6 million young Americans, they outnumber the Baby Boomers and have become our largest generation (though Gen Z or Gen Next coming behind them is also huge).

In 2010, the Urban Land Institute sponsored a survey of Gen Y's housing circumstances and future preferences.[1] The goal of the current update was to determine how the Great Recession affected young people's views of housing and to examine their current living situations. With regard to the latter, figure 1 describes just who those folks are, where they are living, how many are working, and the incomes of those with full-time employment.

Key Gen-Y Findings

50 percent are renters. Of those, only 60 percent rent apartments or townhouse-style units; 40 percent rent single-family or mobile homes.

Two-thirds of tenants are very satisfied or satisfied with being renters.

Median rent is only $925 per month, so most cannot afford 21st-century luxury rentals.

Only 13 percent of Gen Yers live in or near downtowns.

21 percent live at home. Most of those 16.5 million young people will eventually move out on their own, initially to rentals.

14 percent live in households containing three generations of family members.

With regard to self-image, 37 percent think of themselves as city people, 36 percent as suburbanites, and 26 percent as small-town or rural folks.

Virtually all expect to own a home eventually, though they are not necessarily convinced that housing is a good investment.

Nine of ten expect to match or exceed their parents' economic circumstances.

In a generation of 78.6 million, any preference of even a small percentage constitutes a lot of consumers.

Generation Y represents the largest source of new demand for rental housing and first-time home purchases.

[1]M. Leanne Lachman and Deborah L. Brett, *Generation Y: America's New Housing Wave* (Washington, DC: Urban Land Institute, 2011).

FIGURE 1: Profile of Surveyed Gen Yers

	Percentage of total sample			Percentage of total sample
Gender			**Marital status**	
Male	49%		Single/divorced/widowed	62%
Female	51%		Married/partnered	38%
Age			**Living with children under age 18**	
19–24	35%		Yes	28%
25–30	33%		No	72%
31–36	32%		**Have a car**	
Race			Yes	83%
White	73%		No	17%
Black	15%		**Typical commuting time, one way**	
Other*	12%		Under 15 minutes	31%
Hispanic origin			15–30 minutes	40%
Yes	22%		31–60 minutes	23%
No	78%		Over 60 minutes	6%
Region of residence			**Parental contribution to living expenses**	
Northeast	17%		None	69%
Midwest	21%		Under 25%	12%
South	37%		25–49%	8%
West	25%		50–100%	11%
Pet owner				
Yes	57%			
No	43%			

*Other racial groups include Asians, Native Americans, Pacific Islanders, and people who identify themselves as biracial or multiracial.

Sample size=1,270, except for income of full-time workers (n=791) and commuting time (n=1,123).

Source: UDR/Lachman Associates Survey, November 2014.

Current Housing

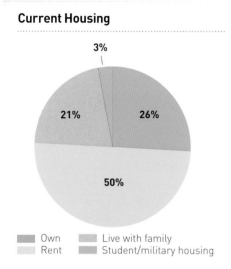

▬ Own		▬ Live with family	
▬ Rent		▬ Student/military housing	

Income of Full-Time Workers

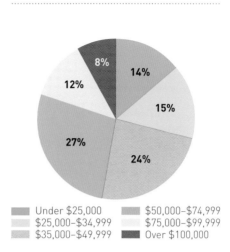

▬ Under $25,000	▬ $50,000–$74,999
▬ $25,000–$34,999	▬ $75,000–$99,999
▬ $35,000–$49,999	▬ Over $100,000

Gen Y's Self-Image

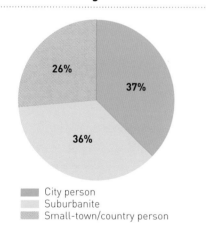

▬ City person
▬ Suburbanite
▬ Small-town/country person

Employment Status

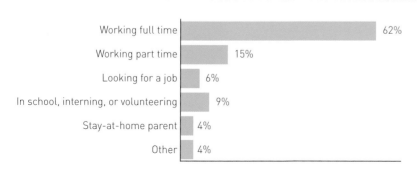

Working full time	62%
Working part time	15%
Looking for a job	6%
In school, interning, or volunteering	9%
Stay-at-home parent	4%
Other	4%

Half of the sample currently rents, well above the 37 percent of four years earlier. The corollary is that only 26 percent are owners—a full ten percentage points below the 2010 figure. That finding suggests that a pause occurred in homebuying over the past several years in the face of housing market turmoil, difficulty in qualifying for mortgages, and possibly a shift to renting among Gen Yers who bought at the market peak. In the ten years from second quarter 2004 to second quarter 2014, the nation's homeownership rate dropped 4.6 percent; but for households under age 35, the decline was 7.7 percentage points.[2]

Rather than purchase houses, Gen Yers rent them—to the extent that 40 percent of Millennial renters live in single-family dwellings, townhouses, duplexes, rowhouses, or mobile homes. (This share matches the 2010 finding.)

Apartment and condominium renters constitute 28 percent of the total sample, and the vast majority live in walkup, two- to three-story buildings. No more than 15 percent of renters are in mid-rise or high-rise elevator buildings. Therefore, most Gen Yers are not among the "multifamily elite" living in amenity-rich in-town buildings featured in the real estate press. However, nearly two-thirds of the apartment renters live in cities—21 percent in or near downtown and 43 percent in city neighborhoods outside downtowns.

A consistency between this survey and previous ones is that only 13 percent of the total sample lives in or near downtown areas. Therefore, even though in-town Millennials are much discussed by journalists, they are not representative of their generation as a whole. As shown in figure 1, when asked to describe themselves:

- 37 percent say they are "city people."
- 36 percent identify as "suburbanites."
- 26 percent are "small-town/country persons."

Among the "city people," three-fourths live in central-city neighborhoods outside downtowns. Even so, a significant contingent of "non-downtowners" is attracted to denser, mixed-use, walkable neighborhoods from which their commute will be short to moderate in length.

To reemphasize a critical point: one-fifth of Gen Yers live at home with their parents or other relatives. Consequently, more than 16.5 million people could be moving out on their own as they become employed in jobs paying enough to support independent living, as they marry or partner, or as they accumulate the downpayment for a home purchase. The majority will rent before owning, so those Millennials represent a promising future demand for America's landlords.

Fully 70 percent of Gen Yers expect to be homeowners by 2020, despite the fact that only 26 percent own today. (The response to this question five years ago was almost as high—67 percent—so the generation's naive optimism remains consistent.) Only 4 percent believe they will still be living with their parents in 2020. Even among those who do not expect to own in five years, 92 percent believe they will eventually purchase homes. Again, that matches the response in 2010.

[2]Robert Dietz, "Homeownership Rate Continues to Decline," *Eye on Housing* (blog), July 29, 2014. http://eyeonhousing.org/2014/07/homeownership-rate-continues-to-decline.

Respondents were asked whether their generation agrees with the traditional American belief in homeownership as a good long-term investment, with the expectation of future value gains. Opinions are mixed: 55 percent agree and 45 percent disagree. Nonetheless, virtually all expect to become owners at some time in the future.

Another measure of Gen Y's positive thinking is the answers to the question "Do you feel that you will eventually be better off economically than your parents?"

- 32 percent expect to be a lot better off.
- 32 percent anticipate being somewhat better off.
- 24 percent say they will be at the same economic level.
- Only 12 percent think they will be worse off.

Among blacks, 38 percent expect to be a lot better off, and only 7 percent think they will be worse off. Hispanics[3] are even more optimistic: 42 percent believe they will be much better off than their parents versus 29 percent of non-Hispanics. (The number of immigrants in the sample is unknown.)

In 2012, the Clark University Poll of Emerging Adults (ages 18–29) found that 77 percent expected to do better financially than their parents. Last summer's release of the Clark University Poll of Established Adults (ages 25–39) showed that 61 percent felt that "overall, their lives will be 'better than my parents' lives have been.'"[4]

Much of this monograph's analysis focuses on preferences among Gen Yers for one type of housing or one location over another. However, it is important to keep in mind that, given the size of this population cohort, a small percentage choosing to do anything translates into a large number of consumers. For example, even if only 9 percent work from home, that is 7.1 million owners or renters who need space for a home office. Similarly, the 13 percent who are "downtowners" represent 10.2 million young people who like living in the urban core.

---

[3]Hispanics can be of any race: white, black, Asian, biracial, or multiracial.
[4]Clark University Poll, www.clarku.edu/clarkpoll.

Gen Y: An Overview

Gen Yers constitute 26.3 million American households, or over one-fifth of the total. The number is rising, as shown in figure 2, and it will continue to do so as more young people achieve independence and gradually move out of their parents' homes. By far, Millennials are the largest source of new demand for rental housing and first-time home purchases.

Household Composition

In the survey, 62 percent of respondents are single, divorced, or widowed, and 38 percent are married or partnered. Those proportions are unchanged since the original 2010 survey—even though the generation is five years older, and many marriages and divorces have occurred. The youngest group of Gen Yers, ages 19 to 24, accounts for nearly 35 percent of the sample, but only 15 percent of them are married or partnered, as reflected in figure 3.

FIGURE 2: U.S. Households under Age 35, 1990–2013

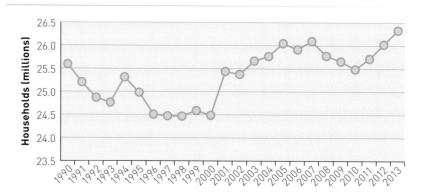

Source: U.S. Census Bureau.

FIGURE 3: Gen Y's Marital Status

Status	Age group			Total sample
	19–24	**25–30**	**31–36**	
Single, divorced, or widowed	85%	60%	41%	**62%**
Married or partnered	15%	40%	59%	**38%**

Sample size=1,270.

Source: UDR/Lachman Associates Survey, November 2014.

More than three-fourths of Gen Yers (76 percent) live on their own. Another 3 percent are in student or military housing. Just over one-fifth (21 percent) live at home with their parents or other relatives, essentially the same as the 20 percent found in 2010. Two of five of those living at home had been independent at one time—at college, in the military, or in a separate residence—before returning to their parents; those "boomerang" kids will be discussed in more detail later.

Over one-quarter (28 percent) of the respondents live with children younger than 18, though the proportions are higher for Hispanics (34 percent) and blacks (35 percent). Again, those figures are consistent with the 2010 findings. As one would expect, the share of households with children rises with age:

Age group	Percentage living with children under age 18
19–24	13%
25–30	24%
31–36	50%

Another contingent (18 percent) lives with roommates to whom they are not related. Among renters, 27 percent have roommates versus only 4 percent of owners. Again, that finding varies markedly by age:

Age group	Percentage living with roommates
19–24	26%
25–30	17%
31–36	9%

When asked why they share their dwellings with roommates, half say they can live in larger or nicer units, and nearly a third say that expense sharing enables them to be in a better or livelier neighborhood. Although 46 percent indicate that it is fun to live with other people, 37 percent say that they could not live independently without sharing expenses. The bottom line, however, is that 58 percent of those with roommates would prefer to live alone.

Even so, among the respondents who do not live with their parents or in student or military housing, only 18 percent actually live alone: 38 percent reside with one other person, and 18 percent live with two; the remaining 26 percent share their home with three or more people. Those figures include children.

Among Gen Yers who do not live with parents, in dorms at school, or on military bases, half are in units with three or more bedrooms. The proportion is much higher—71 percent—for those with children; only 40 percent of those without children are in dwellings with three or more bedrooms. Many of the large residences are single-family attached or detached homes.

Because multigenerational households (three or more generations under one roof) are reportedly on the rise across America, the survey asked about that. The response was that 14 percent of Gen Yers live in such households. If extrapolated to all 78.6 million Millennials, plus or minus 11 million would be in multigenerational households. In many cases, however, more than one Gen Yer is in the household, so they are double counted; nonetheless, the number could be plus or minus 8 percent of U.S. households. This family composition is most common among black respondents (24 percent), followed by 23 percent of Hispanics. The Asian sample is too small to report separately, but multigenerational households are relatively common among Indian American and Chinese American immigrant families. In some large metropolitan areas, homebuilders are creating a product specifically for such occupants.

Regional Geography

Designed to cover the United States, this survey's representation in the four census regions (Northeast, Midwest, South, and West) matches the national Gen-Y population distribution. Most results do not vary significantly among regions, but one exception is car ownership.

Much has been written about Gen Y's indifference to automobiles: getting driver's licenses later, if at all; viewing cars as utilitarian, not as status symbols; and driving far fewer miles per year than previous generations.[5] Although those trends apply overall, respondents still consider garages and covered parking as important residential amenities.

Of the total sample, 83 percent own automobiles. In the Northeast, the share is only 74 percent; in the West, it is 80 percent. In the Midwest, 85 percent have cars, and the highest ownership (88 percent) is in the South. Gen Y is attracted to a variety of shared auto services: 15 percent report using Zipcar or other car-sharing systems, and another 22 percent say they would avail themselves of such options if they existed in their communities. Uber, Lyft, and so forth have cachet and are expanding in suburban areas where taxis are scarce or nonexistent. Before long, we will see more sharing of personal cars among households in apartment communities and residential neighborhoods—and Millennials will be in the vanguard.

Location: Preferences and Current Place of Residence

As highlighted in the summary, 37 percent of Gen Yers identify as "city people," and an equal share (36 percent) say they are "suburbanites." The others consider themselves "small-town" or "country" people. That self-characterization does not vary significantly by age; however, figure 4 portrays the sharp variations by ethnicity, with half of the Hispanic respondents and nearly half of blacks identifying as city people. Clearly, many of those respondents grew up in cities and remain there. Other Gen Yers may migrate to cities when they start working full time, but most are attached to the geographies in which they were raised. Friends and family are strong magnets.

Whereas only 37 percent of respondents identify as "city people," almost half actually live within central-city boundaries, including 57 percent of Hispanics and 54 percent of blacks. Among white Gen Yers, 45 percent live in cities, though only one-third identify as "city people." That may reflect residence in such large southern and western cities as Houston and Los Angeles, where many suburban-style communities are technically within the central

[5] See Craig A. Griffi, Joe Vitale, Michelle Drew, Bharath Gangula, and Steve Schmith, "The Changing Nature of Mobility," *Deloitte Review,* Issue 15, July 28, 2014, pp. 56–81.

FIGURE 4: Gen Y's Self-Characterization by Race and Ethnicity

Self-characterization	Hispanic	Black	White	Total
City person	51%	47%	33%	**37%**
Suburbanite	31%	35%	37%	**36%**
Small-town or "country" person	18%	18%	30%	**26%**

Sample size=1,270.

Source: UDR/Lachman Associates Survey, November 2014.

FIGURE 5: Current Location of Respondents

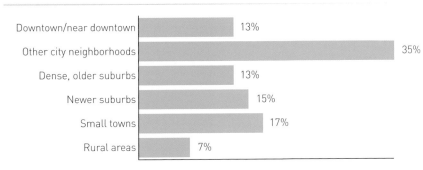

Downtown/near downtown	13%
Other city neighborhoods	35%
Dense, older suburbs	13%
Newer suburbs	15%
Small towns	17%
Rural areas	7%

Sample size=1,270.

Source: UDR/Lachman Associates Survey, November 2014.

city. As figure 5 illustrates, most city dwellers live in city neighborhoods outside of downtown. Also, suburban residents are split between older and newer communities, the former typically being denser than the latter.

A consistent finding in the Gen-Y studies is that only 12–14 percent live in America's downtowns. In this survey, that number is 13 percent. Men are more likely to live downtown: 17 percent of all male respondents versus 10 percent of females. More "downtowners" have roommates (29 percent) than in the overall sample (just under 18 percent), which is probably a result of higher rents in downtown buildings. A logical corollary is that 73 percent of those living downtown are single, compared with 62 percent in the generation overall. Another marked difference is that one-quarter of the downtown residents do not own cars versus 17 percent of Gen Yers as a whole. Almost three-fourths of city-center residents work full time (versus 62 percent overall), and their median earnings are a tad higher (but still less than $50,000 per year).

Both the 2010 housing survey and ULI's 2013 examination of Gen Y's retail preferences,[6] as mentioned, found the same relatively small proportion of "downtowners." We believe that a significant share of those respondents reside in about ten downtowns with large residential populations, retail amenities, cultural attractions, and educational institutions: Boston, New York, Philadelphia, and Washington, D.C., in the Northeast and Mid-Atlantic; Chicago and perhaps Minneapolis in the Midwest; and Denver, Portland, San Francisco, and Seattle in the West. The ULI retail survey discovered that "downtowners" eat out frequently, love to shop, and consider themselves trendsetters. They are the Millennials whom journalists enjoy profiling as typical of their generation; however, when you look at where Gen Yers actually live, the downtowners are clearly atypical.

Many Gen Yers live in central cities—but not necessarily downtown. Because Millennials value walkability and mixed-use neighborhoods, they gravitate toward denser settings than exist in outlying suburbs.

Employment

Of the 1,270 respondents, 791 (62 percent) work full time. In this survey and in 2010, 15 percent of respondents are employed part time. Another 9 percent are attending school, interning, or volunteering. With respect to employment, there are marked differences by age:

- Only 40 percent of those ages 19 to 24 work full time. That is not surprising, because many are still in school.
- 72 percent of those ages 25 to 30 have full-time jobs.
- 76 percent of 31- to 36-year-olds are employed full time.

The job market has improved considerably since the 2010 survey: 14 percent were job hunting then versus 6 percent in 2014. Nevertheless, 27 percent of today's Gen Yers who work either full time or part time feel they are underemployed.

Only 9 percent of respondents work from home every day—fewer than the Millennial literature often implies. Another 12 percent work from home one or two days a week. Therefore, one-fifth could be interested in having a discrete office space at home. Eight of ten respondents seldom, if ever, work from home, though some might use home offices in the evenings or on weekends. Only 11 percent of renters currently have home offices, though 31 percent say such space would be important when considering a new lease.

Finances

Perhaps because of the Great Recession, Gen Yers tend to be cost-conscious and positively thrifty. When asked for a self-description—

- 38 percent say they are "savers."
- 30 percent are "spenders."
- 32 percent claim they can afford to be both.

[6]M. Leanne Lachman and Deborah L. Brett, *Generation Y: Shopping and Entertainment in the Digital Age* (Washington, DC: Urban Land Institute, 2013).

Those in the youngest group are most likely to describe themselves as savers.

When queried about investment accounts with a brokerage firm or other adviser, 22 percent say they have retirement accounts, and 26 percent have other investments; but just over half say they have no remaining money after paying their bills. Even among those in their 30s, 43 percent cannot afford to invest—clearly a factor limiting their ability to buy homes, as will be discussed later.

As indicated before, many more Gen Yers have full-time jobs now than was the case in the 2010 housing survey. Incomes vary widely: 14 percent of respondents who work full time make less than $25,000 per year; however, 20 percent earn more than $75,000. As shown in figure 6, among married or partnered respondents, 45 percent have household incomes exceeding $75,000 per year; only 9 percent earn less than $25,000.

FIGURE 6: Household Income for Married/ Partnered Respondents

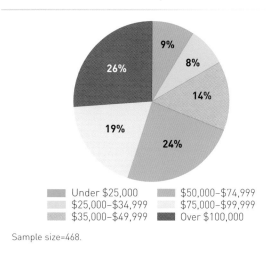

Under $25,000
$25,000–$34,999
$35,000–$49,999
$50,000–$74,999
$75,000–$99,999
Over $100,000

Sample size=468.

Source: UDR/Lachman Associates Survey, November 2014.

Not surprisingly, just under a third of Gen Yers receive help with expenses from relatives (down a bit since 2010). Among those getting financial support, the proportions are as follows:

- 40 percent receive less than 25 percent of their expenses from parents or others.
- 24 percent get 25–50 percent.
- 36 percent reportedly receive support for more than 50 percent of their expenses. They include younger Gen Yers who are still in school.

In order, the most frequently mentioned expenses covered by parents are (a) cellphone bills (thanks to family plans), (b) cable and high-speed internet, (c) health insurance premiums, (d) car insurance, (e) clothing, (f) gasoline, and (g) durable goods (e.g., furniture, electronics).

One-third of Millennials receiving parental financial assistance feel very awkward or embarrassed; one-third say they are somewhat embarrassed; and the remaining one-third are not bothered by parental largesse.

Nearly all Gen Yers (94 percent) have a checking account, savings account, or both; however, one-fifth (21 percent) do not use credit cards at all. Another 31 percent have one or more credit cards but pay them off monthly. Among all respondents, 13 percent have outstanding credit card balances of $6,000 or more. Although that may not sound serious, it suggests that over 10 million Gen Yers are carrying significant short-term debt.

FIGURE 7: Student Debt Status

	Number	Percentage of total respondents
Never incurred debt	477	38%
Fully repaid debt	122	10%
With outstanding debt		
Current on loan payments	390	31%
Behind less than 3 months	45	4%
Seriously delinquent/in default	48	4%
Still in school/recent grad	188	15%

Sample size=1,270.

Source: UDR/Lachman Associates Survey, November 2014.

Overall, Gen Yers appear to be a responsible group. Among the renters in the sample, 84 percent have never fallen behind in their rent, and another 11 percent say it has happened only once or twice. Merely 4 percent have ever been evicted for nonpayment of rent or other lease violations. Similarly, just 8 percent of Millennial homeowners have failed to make a mortgage payment; of those, half were merely one month behind.

Media coverage of rising student debt levels has widely characterized it as a significant deterrent to homeownership for Gen Y. The most recent analyses, by ULI, Pew Research Center, and others, suggest that media reports may have overstated the issue, although it is significant for some.

FIGURE 8: Student Debt Load

	Number	Percentage of total respondents
Under $15,000	189	28%
$15,000–$24,999	129	19%
$25,000–$49,999	149	22%
$50,000–$74,999	83	12%
$75,000–$99,999	54	8%
Over $100,000	67	10%

Sample size=671.

Source: UDR/Lachman Associates Survey, November 2014.

In our survey, nearly half (48 percent) have no student debt at all (38 percent never had it, and 10 percent already repaid it), as presented in figure 7. Roughly 15 percent are still in school and so have not yet had to make payments on their debt. Of those with outstanding balances, 28 percent owe less than $15,000, but 30 percent have to repay $50,000 or more. That said, nearly half of Gen Yers with student debts are currently carrying less than $25,000, as summarized in figure 8. That is consistent with the Urban Institute's finding that student debt—for those who have it—averages $27,000.[7]

[7]Sandy Baum, "How much do students really pay for college?" Urban Institute, Washington, D.C., December 5, 2013.

Still-at-Home Gen Yers

One-fifth of the survey's respondents live with parents or relatives other than a spouse. That is the same proportion as in 2010; so despite an improving economy, as many Gen Yers moved back home as moved out of their parents' homes over the past four years. Among this group, geographic locations are nearly equally divided: 36 percent live with their folks in cities, 32 percent in suburbs, and 32 percent in small towns or rural areas. The younger cohort tends to live at home, as shown in the table below.

Which Gen Yers Still Live with Their Parents or Other Older Relatives?

21 percent of all Gen Yers surveyed

36 percent of those ages 19 to 24

19 percent of 25- to 30-year-olds

8 percent of 31- to 36-year-olds

25 percent of blacks and Hispanics

As mentioned, two of every five who live at home moved back after being on their own. When asked the primary reason for returning home:

- 31 percent wanted to save money or pay down debt.

- 15 percent went back to school and could not afford to live independently.

- 12 percent lost their jobs or had their working hours reduced, so they could not pay their rent.

- 8 percent were encouraged to move home to reduce overall family expenses.

- 8 percent were divorced or broke up with partners.

Among those living at home, 40 percent pay rent or make other financial contributions to their families. Also, as described earlier, 14 percent live in multigenerational households. Hence, both they and one or more children live with their parents, or they live with both parents and grandparents.

When asked "what's good" about living with relatives[8]:

- 84 percent of those living at home cite the ability to save money.

- 47 percent say they like being with their parents and siblings, which reflects Gen Yers' typically close relationship with their families.

- 40 percent highlight free meals.

- 29 percent mention proximity to work.

- 22 percent say they can spend more on entertainment or travel.

[8]Among eight choices, respondents could choose up to three.

With regard to what they "don't like" about living at home, they could identify up to three negatives, and the highest ranking responses are:

- Not enough privacy (62 percent)
- Too many questions/arguments (40 percent)
- "I feel like a failure" (32 percent)

When queried on what would trigger a move out of their parents' home, 40 percent say "when I get a full-time job that pays enough for me to pay rent." The next most frequent reason is marriage or moving in with a partner (18 percent), followed by graduating from college or finishing his or her education (16 percent).

From the parents' perspective, the good news is that only 10 percent expect to be living with their families in five years. Forty percent anticipate renting their own units by then, and 50 percent see themselves as homeowners.

Gen Y's Rental Housing

Half of all Gen Yers live in rental units; but as shown in figure 9, only 60 percent of renters are in apartments or condominiums. Another 3 percent rent a mobile home. The remainder— a very significant 38 percent—are in houses. That finding reflects a nationwide shift in rental options over the past ten years.

FIGURE 9: Rented Units by Structure Type

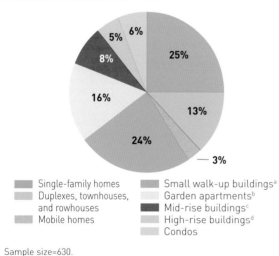

- Single-family homes
- Duplexes, townhouses, and rowhouses
- Mobile homes
- Small walk-up buildings[a]
- Garden apartments[b]
- Mid-rise buildings[c]
- High-rise buildings[d]
- Condos

Sample size=630.

[a]2–6 units, 2–3 stories. [c]4–8 stories.
[b]2–3 stories, no elevator. [d]8 stories or taller.

Source: UDR/Lachman Associates Survey, November 2014.

Traditionally, year in and year out, about one-quarter of America's rental stock consisted of single-family homes. As a result of the recent housing finance debacle, however, many foreclosed homes and distressed mortgages were acquired by investors— ranging from individuals who bought one or two houses that they make available for rent, to large companies like Blackstone and Colony Capital that acquired thousands of homes. Several single-family real estate investment trusts have been formed, many managing rental homes in multiple metropolitan areas.

Census Bureau estimates suggest that houses and mobile homes represent 39 percent of today's rental stock.[9] This survey corroborates those estimates (41 percent of respondents rent single-family detached or attached units, or mobile homes) and reflects the increasing importance of rental single-family units.

[9]U.S. Bureau of the Census, "American Housing Survey: 2013," table C-01-AO.

FIGURE 10: Time Living in Current Rental Unit

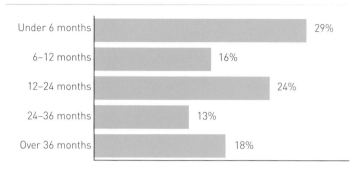

Sample size=630.

Source: UDR/Lachman Associates Survey, November 2014.

Before discussing apartment and house renters separately, several questions that were asked of both groups are worth addressing. Of particular interest is how often Gen Yers move: nearly half (45 percent) of the 630 renters moved at least twice in the past three years, and one-third moved once in that time. Just one of five stayed in place for three years. High turnover among young adults is common. Figure 10 portrays respondents' length of stay in their current rental units. "Downtowners" were least likely to have "stayed put" during the previous three years; only 31 percent live in the same place, compared with 49 percent of those in other urban neighborhoods and 57 percent in older suburbs.

Respondents were asked for up to three reasons for their last move. Of the 18 possible reasons offered, the most frequently selected are:

- Wanted more space/privacy (24 percent).
- Started my first full-time job or changed jobs (24 percent).
- Got married or moved in with a partner (19 percent).
- Wanted to live in a neighborhood that better fits my lifestyle (14 percent).
- Rent was increased or was too expensive where I lived previously (13 percent).
- Started undergraduate or graduate school (10 percent); finished school (another 10 percent).
- Just wanted to try something different (10 percent).

Similarly, the survey asked about the appeal of renting and offered ten options. People could select up to three. The responses, which appear in figure 11, offer no surprises: the key draws are the fact that landlords are responsible for repairs and maintenance, and tenants' ease of mobility (i.e., not being geographically tied down by ownership).

FIGURE 11: Appeal of Renting

	Number selecting each factor	Percentage selecting each factor
Management handles repairs and maintenance	409	65%
Flexibility in how long I stay	356	57%
No long-term commitment to unit or location	293	47%
Renting is more affordable	178	28%
Money not tied up in a residence	157	25%
My credit isn't good enough to buy	120	19%
Roommates help pay rent	111	18%
Appealing amenities (pool, gym, social spaces)	110	17%
Enjoy socializing in my building/apartment complex	62	10%
Concerned about job security	71	11%

Sample size=630.

Source: UDR/Lachman Associates Survey, November 2014.
Note: Respondent could select up to three factors.

Two-thirds are very satisfied or satisfied with being renters. The remainder say they would prefer to own, but renting is currently the best alternative for them or their families. Only 11 percent have applied for a home mortgage, and were rejected and are therefore renters by default.

Apartment Rentals

Among units occupied by the respondents, two-thirds are in two- to three-story garden apartment or small walkup buildings (defined as containing two to six units or in buildings with two to three stories). Condominiums account for 6 percent of rentals. Only 8 percent of the units are in mid-rise (four to eight stories) elevator buildings, and an even smaller 5 percent are in high-rise buildings. Hence, as shown in appendix figures B-1 and B-2, few respondents live in amenity-rich apartment communities or luxury units targeting the "multifamily elite."

With a median monthly rent of $925, the average Gen Yer cannot expect abundant amenities. Among the renters who answered the question about rent paid (n = 455)[10]:

■ 27 percent pay less than $700 per month.

■ 30 percent pay between $700 and $999.

■ 31 percent pay between $1,000 and $1,599.

■ 12 percent pay over $1,600.

[10]Does not include respondents renting single-family detached or mobile homes.

For three out of ten, heat is included in the rent. Among other items covered by rent:

■ Trash is collected for 67 percent.

■ 57 percent get cold water; 35 percent receive water heating.

■ 55 percent have sewer service included.

■ 15 percent of rents include air conditioning.

Responses to the question about paying for covered parking are shown in figure 12. Basically, 18 percent already pay, and another 27 percent would be willing to pay if covered parking were available. (Later, when asked about important amenities, 48 percent cited covered parking.)

Two-thirds get cable TV, but only 15 percent have basic cable service included in their rent. In keeping with evolving communications technology, 26 percent of renters say they can watch shows and news broadcasts on their computers or phones and do not need cable. However, they do need the internet.

For 7 percent of renters, high-speed internet is included in their rent. All those in multitenant buildings were asked whether they would pay extra for super high-speed internet service (in excess of 100 megabits per second). Opinions were mixed:

■ 36 percent said yes.

■ 43 percent said maybe, depending on cost.

■ 21 percent said no.

The oldest respondents were most likely to say yes (42 percent), compared with 30 percent of those ages 25 to 30, and 38 percent of the 19- to 24-year-olds. The latter are most addicted to the internet and are most likely to be receiving parental support in paying for their connections.

FIGURE 12: Willingness to Pay for Garage Parking

Already pay	18%
Willing to pay, but not available	27%
Can use free off-street parking	26%
Can park on the street	17%
Don't have a car	12%

Sample size=455.

Source: UDR/Lachman Associates Survey, November 2014.
Note: Does not include renters in single-family/mobile homes.

The survey asked whether apartment and townhouse renters would pay extra for such ecofriendly features as energy-saving appliances or heating, ventilating, and air-conditioning systems; water conservation; recycled materials in roofing, flooring, and cabinets; and so forth. The 455 responses are distributed as follows:

- 35 percent like the idea but are not willing to pay more.
- 25 percent would pay up to 5 percent more in rent.
- 13 percent would pay 5–10 percent more.
- 3 percent would pay more than 10 percent extra.
- 24 percent say that is not a primary concern.

Bottom line: 41 percent will pay more for "green."

Fewer than half the apartment and townhouse renters live in properties with a full-time onsite manager. Even so, one-third are "very satisfied" with their landlords or property management companies, and over half are "satisfied." Just 15 percent are "dissatisfied."

When asked how they communicate with management, the apartment dwellers responded as follows (with multiple answers allowed):

- 88 percent by telephone
- 65 percent by e-mail
- 61 percent by visiting the management office
- 29 percent in writing
- 24 percent using the management firm's website

One-third of apartment and townhouse renters said they have no way to communicate electronically with management or with other tenants, but a majority use their computers, tablets, or smartphones to perform a variety of apartment-related functions, as shown in the table below.

How Gen Yers Use Electronic Media to Communicate with Property Management
46 percent to pay rent
42 percent to report a maintenance or service need
20 percent to be alerted to upcoming maintenance
18 percent to sign a lease
16 percent to hear about social activities/events
15 percent to renew a lease
12 percent to be notified of package arrival

Millennials place a high value on proximity to friends and family—to the extent that 20 percent of the apartment renters had friends or relatives living in the same building or complex when they made the decision to rent. Among Hispanics, the share is 29 percent; for non-Hispanics, it is 17 percent.

Single-Family Rentals

The 259 renters who occupy single-family houses and mobile homes were asked why they chose those freestanding units. Ten possible reasons were posed, and respondents could select as many as they thought were relevant. Nearly 45 percent cite "more privacy," and 41 percent like having a backyard. About 31 percent believe they get more interior space for the money, and a similar share value the additional storage space. One-quarter say they like having a garage, and 20 percent enjoy their more suburban or rural setting.

Among those renting an entire house or a room within a house, 54 percent are located within cities, 22 percent are in suburbs, and 24 percent are in small towns or rural areas; so there is a strong bias toward cities. (By comparison, the geographic distribution of homeowners is 36 percent in cities, 38 percent in suburbs, and 26 percent in small towns or rural areas.)

Sourcing Rentals

All renters were asked how they found their current unit. (Although the respondents may have consulted multiple sources, they were asked to pick the most important one.) One-third used online resources, such as craigslist, Rent.com, Zillow, Trulia, or Realtor.com. Another 27 percent found their rental by word of mouth, through friends, or through roommates. The positive experiences of tenants past and present are clearly important in reaching new renters. Eight percent used real estate agents, and 7 percent said they looked on a management company website. Such traditional sources as signs, billboards, newspaper ads, and university postings are far less important in attracting Gen-Y tenants. However, people involved in leasing will need to consider a variety of sources when trying to attract young adults.

Gen Y's Ownership Housing

Overall, 26 percent of Gen Yers own their residences and, as expected, owners constitute a higher proportion of older households:

- 8 percent of 19- to 24-year-olds own.
- 25 percent of 25- to 30-year-olds own.
- 47 percent of 31- to 36-year-olds own.

The line that "age 30 is what 20 used to be" applies to a lot of Gen Yers. Many marriages now occur in the early 30s, often followed quickly by children, home purchases, and general "settling down." Some say they are making the life choices in their 30s that their parents made when they were twentysomethings.

In the sample, 29 percent of white respondents are homeowners, whereas that is true of only 14 percent of blacks and 20 percent of respondents of all other races.[11] One in five Hispanic Gen Yers are owners, compared with 28 percent of non-Hispanics. Homeownership rates for minorities have traditionally been lower than for whites regardless of age, and that pattern holds true in the younger generation.

[11] This group includes biracial or multiracial Gen Yers in the sample.

FIGURE 13: Gen Y's Homeownership Units

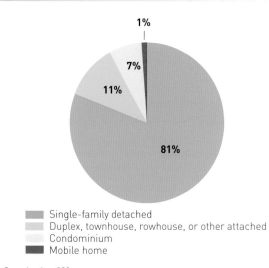

1%

7%

11%

81%

■ Single-family detached
■ Duplex, townhouse, rowhouse, or other attached
■ Condominium
■ Mobile home

Sample size=329.

Source: UDR/Lachman Associates Survey, November 2014.

For three-quarters of owners, their current residence is their first ownership experience. Among those who owned previously, most consider today's residence a "move up." Eight out of ten owners live in single-family homes, as reflected in figure 13, and 11 percent have a duplex, townhouse, rowhouse, or other attached unit. Just 7 percent are in condominiums, and 1 percent own mobile homes. Differences in location also exist: nearly one in four owners living in or near downtowns bought in condominium buildings with four or more stories.

Over one-fifth of owners (22 percent) bought a newly built home. The entire set of respondents was asked how important it would be to live in a brand new home, apartment, or condominium in the next five years. Only 22 percent consider new construction to be very important—presumably many of the same people who already acquired a new house. Another 36 percent say it is somewhat important, and the remaining 42 percent say that "brand new" is unimportant.

When asked about their motivations for buying a home, with each respondent able to select up to three reasons from a list of 14, the results are—

- Owning a home is a good long-term investment (46 percent).
- Owning a home offers stability and certainty (41 percent).
- I/we wanted more space and more privacy (40 percent).
- Housing prices were low/depressed during/after the recession, so I/we wanted to take advantage of the opportunity to build equity (26 percent).
- I got married or moved in with a partner (15 percent).

Nearly half (47 percent) of the Gen-Y homeowners have lived in their homes for more than three years. Although the survey did not separately identify owners with four to eight years of tenure, some undoubtedly purchased their homes during the "peak" prerecession years. Another 15 percent have owned their homes for two to three years. Two out of five homeowners made the decision to buy less than two years ago—after the economy was on the mend.

Gen-Y owners paid an average of $275,859 for their current homes. The highest average price was registered in newer suburbs ($356,604), followed by downtowns at $337,232; the lowest average was $146,947 in rural areas. Because they have ridden the real estate roller coaster since becoming homeowners, respondents were asked how their properties have performed over time. Over half the owners (56 percent) believe their home values have risen since they bought, and 27 percent think they have remained flat. Notably, 17 percent think their home value has dropped. However, when asked if they owe more on their mortgage than the home is worth, only 8 percent said yes.

To determine how they financed their purchase, the survey offered respondents eight possible downpayment sources. Multiple responses were possible. Three-fourths say they used "money I/we saved from wages, salary, and/or investments." A distant second, mentioned by only 15 percent, is "gifts from parents or other relatives, in total or in part," and another 5 percent obtained a loan from a relative. Only 7 percent participated in a government incentive program offering downpayment assistance. More (10 percent) used equity from the sale of a prior residence.

Three-quarters of the owners have 30-year first mortgages. Over one-third (36 percent) had to buy private mortgage insurance. With regard to interest rates:

- 36 percent pay under 4 percent.
- 31 percent pay 4 to 5 percent.
- 15 percent pay 5 to 6 percent.
- 9 percent pay 6 to 7 percent.
- 9 percent pay over 7 percent.

The average interest rate for all homeowners in the sample is 4.4 percent. Only 12 percent of borrowers have an adjustable-rate mortgage. Nearly one in five received prepurchase homeownership counseling, either from their lender, real estate agent, or a government or nonprofit agency. Why the 18 percent who are paying over 6 percent in interest have not refinanced is unknown.

Satisfaction with Homeownership

Figure 14 illustrates Gen Y's strong satisfaction with homeownership—among the 26 percent who have acquired residences. Slightly more men than women say they are "very satisfied," but the difference is not statistically significant. In answers to other questions, women worry more about a possible job loss than men do. Also, a higher proportion of women say that owning a home has ended up being more expensive than anticipated.

FIGURE 14: Satisfaction with Ownership

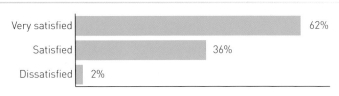

Very satisfied	62%
Satisfied	36%
Dissatisfied	2%

Sample size=329.

Source: UDR/Lachman Associates Survey, November 2014.

When asked what they like most about homeownership—with the ability to choose up to three attributes out of ten—the results are not surprising (see table below).

Gen Yers' Top Five Homeownership Attributes

Building equity; not paying rent—60 percent

More control over my space—58 percent

More privacy—41 percent

More room—31 percent

Feel more settled—31 percent

On the flip side, though, there is less unanimity in Gen Yers' dislikes about homeownership. Again, they could select up to three complaints from a list of nine. The five most common responses are as follows:

- Don't know how to do necessary maintenance and repairs—31 percent.
- Don't have time to do work around the house/condo—29 percent.
- Worry about what will happen if I/we lose our job(s)—26 percent.
- Won't be easy to sell if I/we want to move—22 percent.
- Being a homeowner costs more than I thought it would—20 percent.

Owners also had an opportunity to comment on the most positive features of their residential location/neighborhood. From a list of 14 attributes, each respondent could select up to three. The six dominant "pluses," in descending order, are:

- Stable and safe neighborhood—64 percent
- It's quiet—36 percent
- Good schools—27 percent
- Close to work; my commute is short—19 percent
- Attractive houses—18 percent
- Walkable neighborhood—18 percent

Sourcing Home Purchases

As with renters, the survey asked homeowners how they identified their current dwellings. Nearly half (47 percent) used a real estate agent, and 16 percent employed an online source, such as Trulia, Zillow, Realtor.com, or craigslist. (Most of those who used a website with real estate agent–sponsored listings to find their home probably used an agent at some point during the purchase process, even if they were not initially represented by one.) One out of ten saw a for-sale sign while driving or walking the neighborhood, 8 percent heard about the home from a friend or relative, and 7 percent looked at the builder's website. Fewer than 2 percent were attracted by a newspaper or magazine advertisement.

Millennial Attitudes and Future Expectations

Regardless of current tenure or housing type, seven of ten Gen Yers believe they will live in detached or attached single-family homes five years from now. As illustrated in figure 15, only 28 percent expect to be in multifamily buildings, and just one-third of those envision living in mid- or high-rise structures. Those forward-looking predictions are virtually identical to the 2010 survey, so the Great Recession has not dimmed Gen Y's preference for single-family homes, mostly detached.

To further probe attitudes toward homeownership, all 1,270 respondents were asked whether they, their spouses, parents, siblings, or grandparents had been subject to a foreclosure. Significantly, 11 percent had that experience in their families, and of the 329 current owners in the sample, only five (fewer than 2 percent) had experienced a foreclosure personally. Among minority respondents, the share with personal or family experiences of foreclosure is higher: 17 percent among blacks and 16 percent among Hispanics, compared with 10 percent among whites and non-Hispanics. Surprisingly, a majority of those with personal or family foreclosure experience still believe that homeownership is a good long-term investment (55 percent)—the same share as the sample as a whole.

Fully 70 percent of survey participants expect to be homeowners by 2020—even though only 26 percent currently own. A truism of survey research is that respondents are notoriously poor predictors of the future. In 2010, 67 percent of Gen Yers—and 75 percent of the people who would be in their 30s now—expected to be owning residences in 2015. Not even half have achieved that goal, but their hopes remain high for five years in the future. Similarly, 21 percent live with their parents now—the same proportion as four years ago—yet only 4 percent think they will still be living at home in five years.

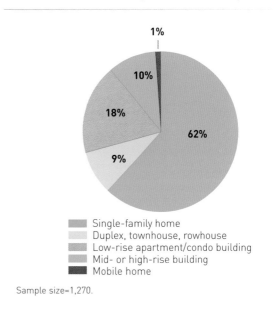

FIGURE 15: Gen Y's Expected Homes by 2020

1%
10%
18%
62%
9%

- Single-family home
- Duplex, townhouse, rowhouse
- Low-rise apartment/condo building
- Mid- or high-rise building
- Mobile home

Sample size=1,270.

Source: UDR/Lachman Associates Survey, November 2014.

The survey asked the 870 respondents who do not own today how they expect to generate the eventual downpayment for a home purchase. They could identify multiple sources:

■ 85 percent say they will use money saved from their paychecks, investments, or both.

■ Only 10 percent expect to rely on funds from parents or other relatives.

■ 17 percent say they could combine their savings with contributions from family members.

■ 6 percent anticipate inheritances.

■ 5 percent say they can use incentives from their employer or that of a spouse or partner.

■ 7 percent admit they do not know where the downpayment will come from.

Given Gen Y's desire for homeownership and the positive comments that current owners make about homeownership's investment potential, equity creation, and so forth, it is surprising to find Millennials largely neutral about residential investment prospects. The survey asked, "If you had a large sum of money to invest today, how would you rate housing/homeownership as an investment?" The answers were as follows:

- Very positively: 15 percent

- Somewhat positively: 34 percent

- Neutral: 37 percent

- Somewhat negatively: 11 percent

- Very negatively: 3 percent

Though the responses are certainly more positive than negative, this is hardly a ringing endorsement. Gen Y may well be fiscally realistic. One assumes that the psychological benefits of ownership (being settled, secure, stable, in control) are as important as investment results. Also, Gen Yers (like their parents) appreciate the extra space, the backyard, and the privacy that usually come with homeownership.

One of the greatest predictors of when consumers change their housing circumstances is a change in their stage of life. The fact that many are marrying and having children later plays a role in when they choose to buy a home. . . . Some have suggested that the decline in younger homebuyers represents a permanent change in preferences. But the evidence points to the economy and access to credit as equally important factors. As the economy improves and as they move through various phases of their lives, their housing preferences are likely to shift as much as it did for previous generations.

GREGG LOGAN, "MILLENNIALS' INFLUENCE ON NEW HOME DEMAND," *THE ADVISORY,* RCLCO, NOVEMBER 6, 2014

The survey asked all respondents to identify the community features that will be most important to them when they choose a neighborhood in which to reside in five years. Out of 13 choices, each Gen Yer was asked to rank his or her five most essential features. Figure 16 shows how many people placed each community feature in their top five and also how many number one votes each feature received.

In considering a future residential community, cost of housing is the most important factor—ranked among the five critical features by 85 percent of Generation Y and considered number one by 42 percent. Neighborhood safety is among the top five criteria for 73 percent of Generation Y, and proximity to work is of similar import. One can infer that commuting time is decidedly a Gen-Y concern. Community character, including ambience and visual appeal, is a strong fourth in the top five rankings.

None of the other ten choices is in the top five for a majority of Generation Y, but that does not make them unimportant. "Proximity to family and friends" places fifth. That kind of social allegiance is one of Generation Y's defining characteristics. Another is their strong

FIGURE 16: Relative Future Importance of Residential Community Features

Community Feature	Number ranking feature No. 1	Number ranking feature in top five
Cost of housing	510	1,042
Neighborhood safety	183	894
Proximity to work	131	856
K–12 school quality	118	435
Community character, ambience, and visual appeal	100	628
Proximity to family and friends	60	500
Small town/rural setting	33	181
Urban setting	25	152
Proximity to shopping, dining, and entertainment	18	470
Suburban setting	18	214
Walkability	17	287
Availability of mass transit	8	201
Parks and recreation opportunities	4	265

Sample size=1,225.

Source: UDR/Lachman Associates Survey, November 2014.

Note: Not answered by 45 who still expect to be living with parents in five years.

interest in entertainment, so it is no surprise that "proximity to shopping, dining, and entertainment" ranks sixth overall. School quality is hugely important to those with children—as reflected by its fourth position in the number one rankings.

Among the community features listed in the choices for this question are the three geographies by which respondents were asked to self-identify: urban, suburban, and small town/rural. Here, they were asked where they would envision themselves living five years out, and "suburban setting" takes precedence, followed by "small town/rural setting"; an "urban setting" is definitely in third place. No matter the geography, though, "walkability" is among the top five features for almost one-fourth of Gen Yers. That response argues for relatively dense communities, wherever they are situated.

The survey also requested that respondents identify the five housing features/attributes that will be most important when they choose a residence in five years. Then, it asked them to rank their selected attributes on a scale of one to five. As itemized in figure 17, they were offered ten housing features from which to choose.

FIGURE 17: Important Future Housing Characteristics

Community Feature	Number ranking feature No. 1	Number ranking feature in top five
Purchase price or monthly rent	844	1,130
Interior design/layout/style	92	805
Interior space/square footage	90	920
Building/home security	68	662
Lot size/privacy	63	688
Age of home/building	21	472
Garage	15	426
Building or property amenities/facilities	13	418
Green features and sustainability	11	209
Parking availability	8	391

Sample size=1,225.

Source: UDR/Lachman Associates Survey, November 2014.
Note: Not answered by 45 who still expect to be living with parents in five years.

Once again, cost considerations dominate, with almost 70 percent rating "purchase price or monthly rent" as the most important factor in selecting a residence. Other features received many second- and third-place votes. For example, "interior space/square footage" is ranked number two by 353 Gen Yers and number three by another 226; overall, three-quarters place interior space in their top five attributes.

"Parking availability" and "having a garage," taken together, received top five rankings by two-thirds of the respondents. Almost as many included "interior design/layout/style" among their top five.

The number ten attribute—the one receiving the least support—is "green features and sustainability." That is consistent with renters' responses to the question about their willingness to pay more for ecofriendly features in their apartment community. Only 16 percent were willing to pay 5 percent or more in higher rent to get those features. Thirty-six percent liked the idea in theory but would not pay more, and 24 percent were honest and said that ecofriendly features were not their concern. Homebuilders, landlords, and leasing agents need to be able to demonstrate to their Gen-Y customers that those features have payback in lower utility costs (or other savings), reduced maintenance needs, or increased comfort.

Appendix A: 2014 Survey Methodology

To understand Generation Y's current and anticipated housing preferences, Lachman Associates LLC designed an online survey administered by Research Now to a nationally representative panel of Americans ages 19 to 36. The panel was selected to reflect Generation Y's age distribution (19–24, 25–30, and 31–36 in 2014), gender, race, Hispanic ethnicity, and geographic distribution among the country's four regions, as defined by the U.S. Census Bureau. The targets for panel selection were made on the basis of the demographic characteristics of Gen Yers as shown in the June 2014 Census Bureau estimates.[12] Figure A-1 shows how the final sample (1,270 respondents) compares with the census targets; the sample closely reflects Generation Y's composition. Statistical analyses found that, in every case, the observed difference in percentages fell well within the 90 percent confidence interval.

FIGURE A-1: Sample Design Parameters and Actual Respondent Demographics

	Survey respondents	Census Bureau estimates	Difference
Gender			
Male	49.4%	50.8%	–1.3%
Female	50.6%	49.2%	1.3%
Age			
19–24	34.6%	34.5%	0.0%
25–30	33.0%	33.3%	–0.3%
31–36	32.4%	32.2%	0.3%
Race			
White alone	73.6%	74.6%	–1.0%
Black alone	15.0%	14.7%	0.2%
All other	11.4%	10.6%	0.8%
Hispanic origin			
Hispanic	21.5%	20.6%	0.9%
Not Hispanic	78.5%	79.4%	–0.9%
Region			
Northeast	17.4%	17.3%	0.1%
Midwest	20.7%	20.8%	–0.1%
South	37.2%	37.4%	–0.2%
West	24.6%	24.5%	0.1%

Sources: Lachman Associates LLC and Research Now.

Note: Totals may not add up to 100 percent because of rounding.

[12]U.S. Census Bureau, "Population Estimates," www.census.gov/popest/data/national/asrh/2013/2013-nat-res.html. The design parameters for "Region" are from July 1, 2013 (the latest ones available at the start of the survey): www.census.gov/popest/data/state/asrh/2013/SC-EST2013-ALLDATA6.html.

The online survey was conducted over a ten-day period beginning October 28, 2014. Respondents were required to answer all questions. Research Now tabulated the results.

Because it represents Generation Y as a whole, the sample's youngest participants include men and women who have never completed high school, who are recent high school graduates, or who are still completing their undergraduate or postgraduate education. At the older end, it includes Gen Yers who have been in the workforce for ten to 15 years or more. It includes single persons who live alone or with roommates or who still reside with their parents, as well as families with children.

Appendix B: Features in Gen-Y Rental Buildings and Units

FIGURE B-1: Amenities and Features in Gen Y's Rental Buildings

Feature	Percentage with feature in building or complex
Laundry room	32%
Outdoor pool	31%
Pet-friendly policies	31%
Secure building entryway	29%
Covered parking (garage or carport)	27%
Exercise room/gym	25%
Clubhouse, community room, party room	24%
Recycling	24%
Extra storage space (off balcony or patio, or on same floor)	22%
Package receiving area	21%
Children's playground	17%
Walking, jogging, or bike trails	13%
Free wi-fi in common areas	13%
Business/tech center with computers, fax, printer	13%
Trash disposal chute or trash room on the same floor	13%
Elevators	12%
Dog run/dog park/dog-washing facilities	12%
Tennis courts	11%
Whirlpool/hot tub	10%
Basketball court	9%
Garage (accessible without going outdoors)	9%
Big-screen TV/video room with seating	9%
Organized social activities, classes, lectures	9%
Concierge/doorman	7%
Secure indoor bike storage	7%
Ecofriendly design and/or building materials	6%
Indoor pool	4%

Sample size=410.

Source: UDR/Lachman Associates Survey, November 2014.
Note: Includes only those renters in multistory, multibuilding properties.

FIGURE B-2: Features in Gen Y's Rental Units

Feature	Percentage with feature in unit
Individually controlled heat and air conditioning	52%
Dishwasher	44%
Garbage disposal	40%
Balcony or patio	36%
Ample closet space	36%
Medicine cabinet/vanity/closet in bathroom	35%
Large windows/lots of natural light	33%
Microwave	31%
In-unit washer/dryer	26%
More than one bathroom	26%
Ice maker in refrigerator	24%
Wood flooring in some or all living spaces	23%
Energy-efficient appliances and HVAC systems	21%
High ceilings (9 feet or higher)	19%
Separate dining room	17%
Utilities included in rent	17%
Breakfast bar	16%
Ceramic-/stone-tiled baths	15%
Granite (or similar material) countertops	13%
Stainless-steel appliances	11%
Room for home office	11%
Fireplace	10%
Pantry	10%
High-quality window treatments	9%
Security features (intercom or on screen)	9%
Shower stall (separate from tub)	6%
Internet and/or basic cable included in rent	6%
Exposed brick	5%

Sample size=455.

Source: UDR/Lachman Associates Survey, November 2014.
Note: Does not include renters in single-family homes or mobile homes.